CHICAGO & NORTH WESTERN RAILWAY 1975 THROUGH 1995

PHOTO ARCHIVE

IN MEMORIAM

PETER LETOURNEAU
1950 – 1997

We dedicate this book as a memorial to our friend, partner, and fellow worker Peter Letourneau, who died driving a 1926 3 litre Bentley, a passion close to his heart. We will miss him and wish him God Speed.

Shawn Glidden, Theresa Piemonte, Rick and Debbie Seymour, Tom Warth

CHICAGO & NORTH WESTERN RAILWAY 1975 THROUGH 1995

PHOTO ARCHIVE

Edited with introduction by
Frank W. Jordan

Iconografix

Photo Archive Series

Iconografix
PO Box 446
Hudson, Wisconsin 54016 USA

Books in the Iconografix Photo Archive Series are offered at a discount when sold in quantity for promotional use. Businesses or organizations seeking details should write to the Marketing Department, Iconografix, at the above address.

Library of Congress Card Number 97-70620

ISBN 1-882256-76-X

97 98 99 00 01 02 03 5 4 3 2 1

Cover photo by Michael Guss

Printed in the United States of America

PREFACE

The histories of machines and mechanical gadgets are contained in the books, journals, correspondence, and personal papers stored in libraries and archives throughout the world. Written in tens of languages, covering thousands of subjects, the stories are recorded in millions of words.

Words are powerful. Yet, the impact of a single image, a photograph or an illustration, often relates more than dozens of pages of text. Fortunately, many of the libraries and archives that house the words also preserve the images.

In the Photo Archive Series, Iconografix reproduces photographs and illustrations selected from public and private collections. The images are chosen to tell a story—to capture the character of their subject. Reproduced as found, they are accompanied by the captions made available by the archive.

The Iconografix Photo Archive Series is dedicated to young and old alike, the enthusiast, the collector and anyone who, like us, is fascinated by "things" mechanical.

C&NW's Western Avenue Yard in St. Paul plays host to three rebuilt SD-9s, May 1977. *Gary Scofield*

INTRODUCTION

In April 1995, the Chicago & North Western Railway was absorbed by the Union Pacific Railroad, thus ending a 147-year-old Midwestern railroading tradition. Within days after the C&NW surrendered its independence, its identity and many of the images so long associated with it began to disappear. The C&NW's "Ball and Bar" heraldry and its yellow and green colors were soon smothered by the armour yellow and gray of the UP. The C&NW's trademark first-generation diesel locomotives were quickly retired. Operations at the huge Chicago Proviso Yard, once the largest freight yard in the country, were scaled-back, as its significance had been diminished by that of the UP's massive North Platte, Nebraska facility. Certain branch lines and remote operations, which had become redundant, were put up for sale, while buildings and various landmarks were scheduled for closure and, in some cases, demolition.

The intent of this book is not to bemoan yet another loss of a Class 1 system. Rather, *Chicago & North Western Railway 1975 through 1995 Photo Archive* celebrates the final 21 years of what was a most diverse and colorful railroad. The Chicago & North Western operated a far-ranging system that sprawled from the coal fields of Wyoming to the busy hub of Chicago, and from the port of Duluth-Superior to St. Louis. The closing decades of the C&NW provided railroading enthusiasts with a chance to witness an exciting variety of motive power. The C&NW, which had purchased some of the first EMD road switchers in the early 1950s, had also helped pioneer AC-traction technology through its purchase of hi-tech General Electric locomotives. Few railroads employed motive power that could rival the sight of first generation EMD GP7s teamed with GE C44-9Ws, as they moved legions of coal, grain, potash, ore, and merchandise trains. (Although this variety of motive power and commodities did reflect the diversity of the C&NW in its waning years, its backbone had become the east-west mainline operation. Running from Fremont, Nebraska to Chicago, it hosted a fleet of piggyback and intermodal traffic and carried bridge traffic that brought the Union Pacific east into Chicago.)

Chicago & North Western Railway 1975 through 1995 Photo Archive provides a taste of what the C&NW was like in its final years of independent operation. As a dominant player in Midwestern Granger railroading, it held a vital and an historic position. Surely, the Chicago & North Western will be missed.

Publication of this book would not have been possible without the contribution of photographs from Robert C. Anderson, Ralph Back, Bob Baker, Mike Cleary, Merle Dick, Roger Durfee, Rob Gottsch, Mike Guss, Hadley Photos, Michael Hoff, Paul Hunnell, Albert Krueger, Erich J. Linser, John Luckfield, Doug Meyer, Bruce C. Nelson, Brian Ottaway, Dan Poitras, Joseph R. Quinn, Chuck Schwesinger, Gary Scofield, J.M. Seidl, Brian Walker, and Fran Weiner. I am particularly indebted to Mike Guss, not just for his contribution of photographs, but also for his sharing his intimate knowledge of C&NW operations. Special thanks to my wife, MaryKay, for her patience and for the hours she spent in the kitchen preparing Class 1 meals for everyone involved in the selection of photographs for the book.

Frank W. Jordan
July 1997

Alco C628 #6711 and General Electric U30C #932 are at Westminster Interlocking, St. Paul, Minnesota, March 2, 1975. The C&NW U30Cs were living on borrowed time, and the C628s were just months away from reassignment to ore service on Michigan's Upper Peninsula. *Ralph Back*

Former Katy F7A keeps company with an F7B and an SD45 at South St. Paul Minnesota, March 8, 1975. C&NW stabled a large population of secondhand F-units that frequently called on the Twin Cites. *Ralph Back*

The C&NW was famous for their Chicago-area commuter trains that operated E and F-units and yellow and green bi-level commuter cars. Here, F7A units 410 and 417 layover at Des Plaines, Illinois, April 10, 1976. *Hadley Photo*

SD40-2 #6850 leads four cab units on the former-CGW main line at Randolph, Minnesota, Spring 1976. The line was deemed redundant and was abandoned, following acquisition of the former Rock Island Spine Line in 1980. *Ralph Back*

The C&NW maintained 20 F7A units fitted with head-end power electrical generators for powering its fleet of bi-level commuter coaches used in the Chicago area. Here, the 406 is at Waukegan, Illinois, April 13, 1976. *J.M. Seidl*

SD40-2 #6856 leads a train at Fond du Lac, Wisconsin, May 17, 1976. *Michael Hoff*

Fairbanks-Morse H12-44 #1071 is switching the North Green Bay yard, as a road freight arrives with SD40-2 #6867 and 6851, May 1976. *Francis J. Weiner*

F7A #417 is westbound at Mayfair Tower, west of downtown Chicago, August 26, 1976. *Joseph R. Quinn*

One of C&NW's locomotive shopping sprees netted them 20 former-Frisco Lines' GP7s through the dealer Precision National. Here, the 4371 keeps company with a former Katy-Baldwin hybrid at North Fond du Lac, November 14, 1976. *Francis J. Weiner*

Former CGW SD40 #922 sits on the point of a long string of power at North Fond du Lac, March 1977. Several lines ran out of North Fond du Lac, and a variety of motive power could be found at the service facility there. *Albert Krueger*

Former-Quebec North Shore and Labrador GP9 #4514 leads a mix of *geeps* and F-units at Randolph, June 1977. *Dan Poitras*

RS36 #405, RS3 #1553, and RSD4 #1517, 1516, and 1515 have cut away from their train to do switching at Brookings, South Dakota, June 5, 1977. *Michael Guss*

RSD5 #1688 is shown switching at Aberdeen, South Dakota, July 1977. The unit was one of three RSD5s to have both steam generator and dynamic brakes, hence the high short hood. Sister units 1686 and 1687 were the other two. *Michael Guss*

F7A #215 and GP9 #4514 are about to pass beneath Dayton's Bluff in St. Paul, July 16, 1977. By this date, the C&NW was down to only a handful of operating F7A units in freight service. *Dan Poitras*

U30C #933 and former-Chicago Great Western (CGW) SW900 #143 were at Chicago & North Western's East Minneapolis, Minnesota yard, September 5, 1977. C&NW's small fleet of U30Cs were based in the Twin Cities, and could commonly be found at work there. Dan Poitras

RSD5 #1689 and three more Alcos bask in the afternoon sun at Brookings, October 16, 1977. All of C&NW's Alco 244-powered engines (RS3, RSD4 and RSD5 models) were retired by mid-1981. *Michael Guss*

Commuter F7As 417, 419, and 418 layover at East Minneapolis, February 23, 1978. On weekends, C&NW often used spare commuter engines to pull its "Viking 400" intermodal train between Chicago and St. Paul. *Dan Poitras*

GP7 #159 hurries a short wayfreight south of Sheldon, Iowa, March 17, 1978. This unit was part of an order of GP7s built for C&NW's subsidiary, Chicago, St. Paul, Minneapolis & Omaha. *Dan Poitras*

Train 482, with C425 #402 on the point, passes the tower at Mankato, Minnesota. The tower protected the crossing of the Milwaukee Road, and was removed shortly after this April 30, 1978 view. *Michael Guss*

GP7 #4386, a former Union Pacific unit, leads an impressive lashup of six GP7s around the curve at Westminster Interlocking in St. Paul, April 30, 1978. The 4386 was part of a 1977 purchase of 25 former-UP GP7s. *Dan Poitras*

SD9 #6603 leads train 495 over the Burlington Northern crossing east of Arlington, South Dakota, June 18, 1978. *Michael Guss*

RSD4 #1619 and RSD5s #1666 and 1690 take a break at Brookings, while battling the aftereffects of a blizzard, January 17, 1979. *Michael Guss*

C&NW operated occasional inspection trains over its system, using a fleet of company-owned business cars to carry officials. Prior to the assignment of former commuter F-units, power for these trains seemed to be drawn from whatever was available, as evidenced by this view of GP35 #830 and GP30 #823 at Merriam, Minnesota, May 5, 1979. *Dan Poitras*

FP7A #217 leads a long consist of F-units and a lone GP9 south of Roseport, Minnesota on the former CGW main line, May 5, 1979. The F-units were in their last year of regular operation. *Dan Poitras*

E8A #522 charges westbound out of downtown Chicago with a long train of bi-levels, July 2, 1979. *Paul Hunnell*

GP35 #831 prepares to depart North Fond du Lac with a Milwaukee-bound freight, August 12, 1979. The second unit, a leased Conrail GP40, would be purchased by the C&NW three years later and become C&NW 5521. *Albert Krueger.*

GP30 #820 and SD9 #6614 lead a long train of 40-foot box cars through Lake Benton, Minnesota, September 1979. The box cars are loaded with Dakota-grown grain bound for eastern markets. *Michael Guss*

SD40 #888 and two GP30s, the second one leased from Conrail, lead a transfer into Western Avenue Yard at St. Paul, September 30, 1979. *Dan Poitras*

Train 482 with SD9 #6614 prepares to depart Sioux Valley Junction, South Dakota, after setting out a cut of cement cars for the cement plant at Watertown, South Dakota. On this October 8, 1979 day, the train's consist included RS32 #4001, leased from used locomotive dealer Chrome Crankshaft, as the fourth unit. *Michael Guss*

SD9 #6613 and RSD5 #1690 lead a short train 495 past the abandoned Peavey elevators at Manchester, South Dakota, November 3, 1979. *Michael Guss*

In late 1979, the C&NW experienced a severe power shortage, and was leasing almost anything they could get their hands on. Two former-Southern Pacific RS32s were leased from Chrome Crankshaft and assigned to the shop at Huron, South Dakota, where they fit right in with C&NW's own Alcos. Here, the 4003 is on the point of train 482 at Sioux Valley Junction. *Michael Guss*

SD40-2 #6832 storms east with a leased Conrail GP35 on the double-track main line near Denison, Iowa, November 17, 1979. At this time, the westbound main track was still jointed rail, while the eastbound main track had been re-laid with continuous welded rail for operation of loaded unit coal trains. *Dan Poitras*

During late 1979, when other major railroads were ridding themselves of Alco power, C&NW made an unbelievable purchase of 10 former-Conrail RS32s. The units, numbered 4240 through 4249, were assigned to work out of Huron, which was home to the C&NW's remaining non-C628 Alco fleet. Here, 4241 leads sister 4244 and a leased Chrome Crankshaft RS32 on train 482 at Brookings, February 1980. *Michael Guss*

Engine 1509, a Baldwin DRS-6-6-1500 repowered with an EMD engine, keeps company with a quartet of Alco C628s at North Green Bay, Wisconsin, February 9, 1980. These hybrid engines were used to switch industries whose tracks were too fragile to handle the big C628s. *Albert Krueger*

GPl5-1 #4413 leads a southbound freight south of Oshkosh, Wisconsin, March 25, 1980. The C&NW owned 25 GPl5s and assigned them to wayfreight service throughout the system. *Albert Krueger*

C425 #402, RS32 #4247, and two SD9s sit at the Brookings depot, June 6, 1980, while the crew is at lunch. *Michael Guss*

Two Alco C628s pull an ore train into the yard at Iron Mountain, Michigan, June 17, 1980. The C&NW purchased 30 of these units from the Norfolk & Western in June 1973. The units originally operated in general freight service, and were based at the Cedar Lake shop in Minneapolis. They were assigned to the ore lines out of Escanaba, Michigan in 1975, when the C&NW retired its fleet of Fairbanks-Morse H16-66 units. *Roger Durfee*

GP35 #857 is in charge of a westbound freight near Chadron, Nebraska, July 8, 1980. The 857 was one of several C&NW GP35s built with oversize fuel tanks, necessitating the placement of the air tanks on the roof. Railfans commonly called these engines "torpedo tube" units. *Michael Guss*

Train 495, with RS32 #4248, takes the siding at Balaton, Minnesota, as train 482, with C425 #402, waits patiently on the main line, July 12, 1980. *Michael Guss*

GP30 #822 and sister 817 at Lake Preston, South Dakota, August 8, 1980. The line between Huron, South Dakota and Winona, Minnesota was known as "the Alco line" until 1981. Nonetheless, EMD visitors were common during harvest season to help move grain extras. *Michael Guss*

Engine 405 at Elkton, South Dakota, February 15, 1981. The locomotive had recently returned to service after several years of storage with a broken crankshaft. Following repair, it had been treated to a fresh coat of paint. The stenciled "gondola" heraldry on the cab would soon be replaced by a standard Scotchlite™ decal. *Michael Guss*

RS32 #4245 leads RSD4 #1516 and RS32 #4247 east of Eagle Lake, Minnesota with train 482, February 25, 1981. *Dan Poitras*

In 1971, C&NW rebuilt the remains of an RS2 and an RS3 into "road slugs", and mated them with their four C425s. A slug is not actually a locomotive but a chassis with traction motors whose power is supplied by parent units. Here, a "slug set" with the 403 leading is east of Balaton, Minnesota, March 3, 1981. *Michael Guss*

Although better known for their fleet of secondhand GP7s and GP9s, the C&NW maintianed a sizable fleet of end-cab switchers. Here, SW1200 #1216 and #1219 are about to enter C&NW's Belt Yard in St. Paul, March 22, 1981. *Dan Poitras*

RS32 #4249 leads train 482 east of Sioux Valley Junction, April 3, 1981. The consist includes RSD4 #1516, making one of its final trips before retirement. The trailing unit is former Rock Island GP7 #4189, making its first trip in C&NW paint. *Michael Guss*

In 1981, the C&NW purchased 120 former-Rock Island GP7 and GP9 units to replace their fleet of aging Alcos assigned to the shop at Huron. Freshly painted 4112 is at Brookings, making its first trip in C&NW colors, April 20, 1981. *Michael Guss*

RS32 #4240 leads former Conrail GP7 #4440 at Sioux Valley Junction, April 1981. *Merle Dick*

SD40 #925 and 928 cross Lake Butte Des Mortes at Menasha, Wisconsin with train 245, May 1981. The two SD40s formerly worked for the CGW, until that road was merged into the C&NW on July 1, 1968. *Albert Krueger*

GP7 #4128 and GP9 #4556, with a long string of cement cars in tow, north of Sioux Valley Junction, May 13, 1981. This train operated between Watertown and Sioux Valley Junction three days a week on a down-one-day-back-the-next type of schedule. *Michael Guss*

HE15 #4252, a GP7 rebuilt with a Cummins engine, leads GP35 #841 around a curve at De Pere, Wisconsin, south of Green Bay, May 19, 1981. The C&NW re-engined two GP7s with Cummins engines in May 1980, and redesignated the model "HE15". These two units enjoyed only limited success and were soon placed in long term storage. *Michael Hoff*

GP7 #4116 leads train 482 west of Brookings on the former "Alco line", May 31, 1981. For many years, most of C&NW's Alco road switchers were based out of Huron. In 1981, when the C&NW purchased a fleet of former Rock Island GP7s and GP9s, the remaining "Huron" Alcos were reassigned to Green Bay, which was home to the C&NW's fleet of Alco C628s. This move eliminated the need to maintain two separate Alco parts inventories. *Michael Guss*

GP7 #4489, with train #290, skirts the shore of Lake Winnebago, on the south side of Oshkosh, Wisconsin, August 1981. *Albert Krueger*

Train 482, with three former Rock Island GP7s, is piloted by a Jordan Spreader, west of Brookings, January 1982. *Michael Guss*

GP7 #4467 leads an eastbound train across the Burlington Northern crossing east of Sioux Falls, South Dakota, June 3, 1982. *Michael Guss*

GP40 #5504, a secondhand unit purchased from Conrail, leads a train through Milwaukee, September 11, 1982.
Michael Hoff

"Torpedo Tube" GP35s #851, 865, and 849 share the service tracks with GP7 #4308, at Chadron, Nebraska, July 1983. *Michael Guss*

In 1973, the C&NW purchased six former Union Pacific E8B and E9B units, and rebuilt them with cabs. These units were called "Crandall Cabs" in honor of Milt Crandall, the late-C&NW Mechanical Superintendent who designed the cabs. Here, the 501 and 502 pose with "as built" E8A #5027A at Des Plaines, Illinois. *Collection of Mike Guss*

Train ALMCA, led by SD40-2 #6890, is on the former Rock Island "Spine Line" at Albert Lea, Minnesota, and is preparing to cross the Soo Line's former-Milwaukee Road line. The brick tower has been closed for many years, with the C&NW's Spine Line dispatcher controlling the crossing. *Michael Guss*

GP7 #4319 leads a freight into North Green Bay, May 26, 1984. The train had made a trip up the valley line from Fond du Lac, and would soon be tying up at the yard in North Green Bay. *Michael Guss*

SD9 #6612 and former Southern Railway SDl8 #6629 switch the small yard at Sioux Valley Junction in July 1984.
Michael Guss

SD40 #887 is on the point of a ballast train at Rock Springs, Wisconsin, August 11, 1984. Rock Springs was home to a rock quarry that supplied most of the railroad with red granite ballast called "pink lady" ballast. *Bruce C. Nelson*

Former-Burlington Northern SD45s 6588 and 6585 pull train RCADA west of Dodge Center, Minnesota, February 7, 1985. The two units eventually received C&NW paint. The former "Alco line" was a good place to find these secondhand SD45s in 1984 and 1985. *Dan Poitras*

SD45 #952 leads a former-Burlington Northern and a former-Conrail SD45 out of the Union Depot in St. Paul, May 2, 1985. With C&NW's many secondhand locomotives, you often had to look twice to see if a unit was a pool unit or something that the C&NW had actually purchased. *Dan Poitras*

GP7 #4205 rides the turntable at C&NW's Harrison Street shop in Minneapolis, as F7A #403 looks on. The GP7 was assigned to Harrison Street for maintenance. The F7A was visiting town on a business train. *Michael Guss*

Former-Burlington Northern SD45 #6585 is on the point of train DWKMA, north of Pine City, Minnesota, May 30, 1986. This line is the former-Northern Pacific "Skally" line, which was not used by Burlington Northern but continued to host trains of the C&NW and Milwaukee Road via trackage rights. *Robert Gottsch*

From 1982 through 1986, the C&NW purchased 114 SD45s from Conrail and Burlington Northern. Some of these units spent their entire C&NW career in the Oelwein, Iowa deadline, before being traded for newer power. Others went on to enjoy many years of service before being retired in 1995. Here, 6472 rides the turntable at Mankato, Minnesota, August 2, 1986. *Erich J Linser*

C628 #6718 with train GBESA waits in the siding at Powers, Michigan, while the caboose of train ESGBA rolls by. *Michael Guss*

SD40-2 #6930 leads an Escanaba-bound ore train around the curve at Partridge, Michigan, August 19, 1986. The Alco C628s, which had ruled supreme on the ore line north of Escanaba, were retired at the end of 1986, and the SD40-2s had become common power on this assignment. *Chuck Schwesinger*

SD40-2 #6863 leads a train heavily laden with intermodal traffic past Tavil Tower at Green Bay, September 4, 1987. *Brian Ottaway*

Nearly new SD60 #8037 leads run-through Soo Line coal train through Newport, Minnesota, October 4, 1987. These big units were primarily used in coal service when new, but quickly found their way into general freight service. *Michael Guss*

GP7 #4146 and 4454 lead a long cut of coal cars past Chestnut Street in downtown St. Paul, October 17, 1987.
Michael Guss

SD45 #6500 leads two Canadian National units on an Iowa-bound potash train at South St. Paul, February 1988. *Michael Guss*

GP7 #4206 leads a Sheboygan, Wisconsin-bound coal train through Butler, Wisconsin in May 1988. The train originated on the Soo Line in Indiana, and the two trailing Soo units will return the train to its point of origin. *Michael Guss*

Train EMPRA, with SD45 #964 on the point, splits the semaphores at Wilson, Wisconsin, June 11, 1988. The line between Hudson and Altoona (Eau Claire), Wisconsin had a nice population of semaphore signals until 1990, when they were replaced with three-color light type signals. *Michael Guss*

For several years, C&NW's former-CGW Robert Street lift bridge in downtown St. Paul sat dormant. The line that crossed this bridge was reopened in 1988 to meet increasing coal traffic. Here, SD40-2 #6847 tests the bridge prior to the line's reopening, August 26, 1988. *Michael Guss*

GP7 #4308 and GP9 #4556 arrive at Belle Fourche, South Dakota, September 12, 1988. The 4308 began life as Minneapolis & St. Louis #607. The 4556 is a former-Rock Island unit. *Chuck Schwesinger*

GP30 #815 and 814 lead a pair of GP35s westbound at Oakdale, Nebraska, September 17, 1988. All four units would be sold to the Fox River Valley Railroad to work former-C&NW trackage in eastern Wisconsin. *Brian Walker*

SD45 #903 leads a pooled Soo Line unit and two C&NW units on train EMPRA at Baldwin, Wisconsin, October 1988. *Michael Guss*

SD60 #8051 prepares to leave Western Avenue Yard at St. Paul, while Soo Line's "Ford Hauler", with two MP15s, passes high above the yard on a spindly wooden trestle. *John Luckfield*

SD45 #6549 still wears Conrail blue, as it shares the facility at East Minneapolis with several other units on Christmas day, 1988. *Michael Guss*

C&NW 3049 was leased from VMV Enterprises. The C&NW leased 14 of these ex-Missouri Pacific SD40s, from late 1988 until mid-1989. Photographed at East Minneapolis, February 12, 1989. *Michael Guss*

GP38-2 #46l9 leads an eastbound train on the double-track main line at Nevada, Iowa, March 11, 1989. *Mike Cleary*

SD40-2 #6916 leads train ITPRA across the Chippewa River at Chippewa Falls, Wisconsin, April 2, 1989.
Michael Guss

On January 1, 1978 the C&NW conveyed operations of its Chicago commuter operations to the Regional Transit Authority (RTA). The sale included all E and F-units except for four F7As retained for use on business trains. Here, F7A #401 (formerly commuter unit #419) leads a business train through the St. Paul Union Depot, July 6, 1989. *Michael Guss*

C40-8 #8526 leads a coal train at Logan, Wyoming, October 4, 1989. The C&NW purchased 30 C-40-8 locomotives in 1989 for use in coal service, and ultimately ended up with 77 of the big units. *Erich J. Linser*

SD40-2 #6926 and 6812 lead unit taconite train ITWCS through East St. Paul, February 4, 1990. During the winter of 1990, the C&NW handled several of these Gary, Indiana-bound unit taconite trains. The trains were interchanged to the C&NW at Itasca, Wisconsin by the Duluth Missabe & Iron Range, and were handed off to the Elgin, Joliet & Eastern at West Chicago. *Michael Guss*

Train EMPRA, lead by a trio of SD40-2s, is one mile east of Roberts, Wisconsin, February 24, 1990. *Michael Guss*

In the 1980s, the C&NW began dispatching its trains using Direct Traffic Control (DTC) in lieu of train orders. The DTC block limits were indicated by wayside signs, and permission to occupy these block limits was granted by the dispatcher via radio. Pictured is train EMPRA leaving the Hersey Block and entering the Tramway Block west of Menominee, Wisconsin, February 24, 1990. *Michael Guss*

SD40-2 #6858 and a pooled Conrail unit lead train EMPRE into Butler, Wisconsin, June 24, 1990. *Bob Baker*

Four SD18s led by the 6640 are on the point of train ALSSA, east of Menominee, Wisconsin, crossing the Red Cedar River. The SD18s were commonly found on wayfreight and yard assignments. It was unusual to see four of them together on the road. *Erich J. Linser*

SD40-2 #6843 and a pooled CSX GP40 lead Fox River Valley Railroad train GBBUA through North Fond du Lac, July 4, 1990. Even after the C&NW sold the line between Milwaukee and Green Bay to the FRVR, C&NW power was still commonly used. *Michael Guss*

As the F-units began to age, their reliability declined, and the new power of choice for business trains became the GP50. Here freshly painted 5075 sparkles in the sun at C&NW's Global-II intermodal facility at Proviso Yard west of downtown Chicago, October 31, 1990. *Bob Baker*

SD50 #7023 leads a coal train at East Minneapolis in July 1991. Today, most of this yard is abandoned, with industrial and commercial buildings standing in place of the tracks. *Frank Jordan*

C40-8 #8554 leads a coal train at Bill, Wyoming, September 18, 1991. *Joe Seidl*

On May 15, 1992, a pair of C-40-8s, with the 8519 on the point, lead train EMPRA through Roberts, Wisconsin. *Robert C. Anderson*

The former Minneapolis & St. Louis shops at Marshalltown, Iowa was once a good spot to view C&NW locomotives, as evidenced by this August 23, 1992 view. Following the merger with the Union Pacific, the shop was deemed surplus, and was closed in the summer of 1995. *Bob Baker*

Four former-Conrail GP40s, with the 5502 on the point, cruise through Faribault, Minnesota with train SSMCA, August 24, 1993. The attractive brick depot, which now serves as a restaurant, can be seen in the background. *Michael Guss*

SD60 #8017 and C-40-8 #8538 lead a Soo Line-bound coal train through Hoffman Avenue Interlocking at St. Paul, on a frigid January 18, 1994. *Michael Guss*

SD40-2 #6816 leads #6859 and train BUMAA south of Bartonville, Illinois, February 13, 1994. The trailing unit on this St. Louis-bound train is a leased former-Santa Fe C-30-7. *Doug Meyer*

SD40-2 #6831 leads an eastbound train over this classic little overpass west of Lake Elmo, Minnesota, February 8, 1994. *Michael Guss*

C44-9W #8602 and sister unit 8625 make a rare appearance on the line north of Escanaba, March 31, 1994. The C&NW tested smaller sister C40-8 units in ore service for a time, but use of the big wide-nosed C44-9W units was extremely short lived. *Chuck Schwesinger*

SD60 #8031 leads an ore train into the yard at Escanaba, March 11, 1994. This train was interchanged to the C&NW by the Wisconsin Central at Hermansville, Michigan. *Chuck Schwesinger*

Engines 6539 and 6523 serve as helper engines, pushing hard on the rear end of train ITPRA at Hudson, Wisconsin, May 25, 1994. To get over Hudson Hill, heavy eastbound trains leaving St. Paul were commonly assigned rear-end pusher power. *Michael Guss*

Train DWPRP is shown entering C&NW trackage at Burlington Northern's Westminster Interlocking in St. Paul, May 1994. The trailing unit is a former-Santa Fe C30-7 leased from General Electric. *Michael Guss*

Three C44-9W units line up and show off their lightning stripes at Bill, Wyoming, June 1994. *John Luckfield*

C-44-9W #8621 leads train BTDYC over the Robert Street bridge in downtown St. Paul, July 20, 1994. This train is bound for interchange to the Burlington Northern, who will handle it to its destination of Alma, Wisconsin. *Michael Guss*

SD18 #6629 and 6622 work the small Southeast Minneapolis yard during the summer of 1994. *John Luckfield*

SD40-2 #6900 is in command of train SSCTU west of Lake Elmo, Minnesota, September 14, 1994. This train is a unit train of coking coal that originated at the Koch Refinery at Roseport, Minnesota. *Michael Guss*

Train BPNAX, with 8721 and 8513, crosses the Mississippi River on Bridge 15 at St. Paul, September 1994. *Michael Guss*

Potash train DWCTP is near Lake Elmo, Minnesota with a pair of C44-9Ws and an SD40-2, March 8, 1995. The SD40-2 is actually a helper engine, and will be cut off on top of Hudson Hill at Sono, Wisconsin. *Michael Guss*

C44-9W #8711 and 8663 are leading unit potash train DWCTP into Knapp, Wisconsin, March 8, 1995. In the spring, potash is a big commodity on the C&NW. Frequent extras are called to handle the increased volume of traffic. *Michael Guss*

C44-9W #8660 leads a leased General Electric "Super 7" locomotive and an SD60 through East St. Paul with unit potash train DWCTP, April 13, 1995. *Michael Guss*

GP38-2 #4615 leads train OSMTA through Gilman, Iowa, May 13, 1995. This line was once part of the Minneapolis & St. Louis main line, but today only exists in bits and pieces. *Robert C. Anderson*

C44-9W #8677 leads a leased General Electric "Super 7" locomotive and two Union Pacific units at Bill, Wyoming in June 1995. *John Luckfield*

SD60 #8055 and SD40-2 #6853 lead an ore train near Sands, Michigan, August 22, 1995. *Chuck Schwesinger*

In 1993 the C&NW began applying "Operation Lifesaver" decals to their newly repainted locomotives. Operation Lifesaver is the railroad industry's grade-crossing accident prevention program, sponsored by various government agencies and, of course, participating railroads. Here, SD60 #8029 and SD18 #6636 spread the word at Escanaba. *Chuck Schwesinger*

C&NW purchased 37 GP40s from Conrail during 1982, and assigned them to mainline freight service. By 1995, as these units began to age and the ranks of GP7s were thinning, the GP40s were put to work at less prestigious jobs such as that of the 5528, holding down the yard and wayfreight job at Marinette, Wisconsin. *Michael Guss*

The Iconografix Photo Archive Series includes:

AMERICAN CULTURE

AMERICAN SERVICE STATIONS 1935-1943	ISBN 1-882256-27-1
COCA-COLA: A HISTORY IN PHOTOGRAPHS 1930-1969	ISBN 1-882256-46-8
COCA-COLA: ITS VEHICLES IN PHOTOGRAPHS 1930-1969	ISBN 1-882256-47-6
PHILLIPS 66 1945-1954	ISBN 1-882256-42-5

AUTOMOTIVE

FERRARI PININFARINA 1952-1996	ISBN 1-882256-65-4
GT40	ISBN 1-882256-64-6
IMPERIAL 1955-1963	ISBN 1-882256-22-0
IMPERIAL 1964-1968	ISBN 1-882256-23-9
LE MANS 1950: THE BRIGGS CUNNINGHAM CAMPAIGN	ISBN 1-882256-21-2
LINCOLN MOTOR CARS 1920-1942	ISBN 1-882256-57-3
LINCOLN MOTOR CARS 1946-1960	ISBN 1-882256-58-1
MG 1945-1964	ISBN 1-882256-52-2
MG 1965-1980	ISBN 1-882256-53-0
PACKARD MOTOR CARS 1935-1942	ISBN 1-882256-44-1
PACKARD MOTOR CARS 1946-1958	ISBN 1-882256-45-X
SEBRING 12-HOUR RACE 1970	ISBN 1-882256-20-4
STUDEBAKER 1933-1942	ISBN 1-882256-24-7
STUDEBAKER 1946-1958	ISBN 1-882256-25-5
VANDERBILT CUP RACE 1936 & 1937	ISBN 1-882256-66-2

TRACTORS AND CONSTRUCTION EQUIPMENT

CASE TRACTORS 1912-1959	ISBN 1-882256-32-8
CATERPILLAR MILITARY TRACTORS VOLUME 1	ISBN 1-882256-16-6
CATERPILLAR MILITARY TRACTORS VOLUME 2	ISBN 1-882256-17-4
CATERPILLAR SIXTY	ISBN 1-882256-05-0
CLETRAC AND OLIVER CRAWLERS	ISBN 1-882256-43-3
ERIE SHOVEL	ISBN 1-882256-69-7
FARMALL CUB	ISBN 1-882256-71-9
FARMALL F–SERIES	ISBN 1-882256-02-6
FARMALL MODEL H	ISBN 1-882256-03-4
FARMALL MODEL M	ISBN 1-882256-15-8
FARMALL REGULAR	ISBN 1-882256-14-X
FARMALL SUPER SERIES	ISBN 1-882256-49-2
FORDSON 1917-1928	ISBN 1-882256-33-6
HART-PARR	ISBN 1-882256-08-5
HOLT TRACTORS	ISBN 1-882256-10-7
INTERNATIONAL TRACTRACTOR	ISBN 1-882256-48-4
INTERNATIONAL TD CRAWLERS 1933-1962	ISBN 1-882256-72-7
JOHN DEERE MODEL A	ISBN 1-882256-12-3
JOHN DEERE MODEL B	ISBN 1-882256-01-8
JOHN DEERE MODEL D	ISBN 1-882256-00-X
JOHN DEERE 30 SERIES	ISBN 1-882256-13-1
MINNEAPOLIS-MOLINE U-SERIES	ISBN 1-882256-07-7
OLIVER TRACTORS	ISBN 1-882256-09-3
RUSSELL GRADERS	ISBN 1-882256-11-5
TWIN CITY TRACTOR	ISBN 1-882256-06-9

RAILWAYS

CHICAGO, ST. PAUL, MINNEAPOLIS & OMAHA RAILWAY 1880-1940	ISBN 1-882256-67-0
CHICAGO&NORTH WESTERN RAILWAY 1975-1995	ISBN 1-882256-76-X
GREAT NORTHERN RAILWAY 1945-1970	ISBN 1-882256-56-5
MILWAUKEE ROAD 1850-1960	ISBN 1-882256-61-1
SOO LINE 1975-1992	ISBN 1-882256-68-9
WISCONSIN CENTRAL LIMITED 1987-1996	ISBN 1-882256-75-1

TRUCKS

BEVERAGE TRUCKS 1910-1975	ISBN 1-882256-60-3
BROCKWAY TRUCKS 1948-1961*	ISBN 1-882256-55-7
DODGE TRUCKS 1929-1947	ISBN 1-882256-36-0
DODGE TRUCKS 1948-1960	ISBN 1-882256-37-9
LOGGING TRUCKS 1915-1970	ISBN 1-882256-59-X
MACK® MODEL AB*	ISBN 1-882256-18-2
MACK AP SUPER-DUTY TRUCKS 1926-1938*	ISBN 1-882256-54-9
MACK MODEL B 1953-1966 VOLUME 1*	ISBN 1-882256-19-0
MACK MODEL B 1953-1966 VOLUME 2*	ISBN 1-882256-34-4
MACK EB-EC-ED-EE-EF-EG-DE 1936-1951*	ISBN 1-882256-29-8
MACK EH-EJ-EM-EQ-ER-ES 1936-1950*	ISBN 1-882256-39-5
MACK FC-FCSW-NW 1936-1947*	ISBN 1-882256-28-X
MACK FG-FH-FJ-FK-FN-FP-FT-FW 1937-1950*	ISBN 1-882256-35-2
MACK LF-LH-LJ-LM-LT 1940-1956 *	ISBN 1-882256-38-7
MACK MODEL B FIRE TRUCKS 1954-1966*	ISBN 1-882256-62-X
MACK MODEL CF FIRE TRUCKS 1967-1981*	ISBN 1-882256-63-8
STUDEBAKER TRUCKS 1927-1940	ISBN 1-882256-40-9
STUDEBAKER TRUCKS 1941-1964	ISBN 1-882256-41-7

* This product is sold under license from Mack Trucks, Inc. All rights reserved.

The Iconografix Photo Album Series includes:

CORVETTE PROTOTYPES & SHOW CARS	ISBN 1-882256-77-8
LOLA RACE CARS 1962-1990	ISBN 1-882256-73-5
McLAREN RACE CARS 1965-1996	ISBN 1-882256-74-3

The Iconografix Photo Gallery Series includes:

CATERPILLAR PHOTO GALLERY	ISBN 1-882256-70-0

All Iconografix books are available from direct mail specialty book dealers and bookstores worldwide, or can be ordered from the publisher. For book trade and distribution information or to add your name to our mailing list contact

Iconografix
PO Box 446
Hudson, Wisconsin, 54016

Telephone: (715) 381-9755
(800) 289-3504 (USA)
Fax: (715) 381-9756

MORE
GREAT BOOKS FROM
ICONOGRAFIX

WISCONSIN CENTRAL LIMITED 1987-1996 Photo Archive
ISBN 1-882256-75-1

CHICAGO, ST. PAUL, MINNEAPOLIS & OMAHA RAILWAY 1880-1940
Photo Archive ISBN 1-882256-67-0

SOO LINE 1975-1992 Photo Archive
ISBN 1-882256-68-9

MILWAUKEE ROAD 1850-1960
Photo Archive ISBN 1-882256-61-1

GREAT NORTHERN RAILWAY 1945-1970
Photo Archive ISBN 1-882256-56-5

COCA COLA: ITS VEHICLES IN PHOTO-GRAPHS 1930-1969 Photo Archive
ISBN 1-882256-47-6

LOGGING TRUCKS 1915-1970
Photo Arhive ISBN 1-882256-59-X

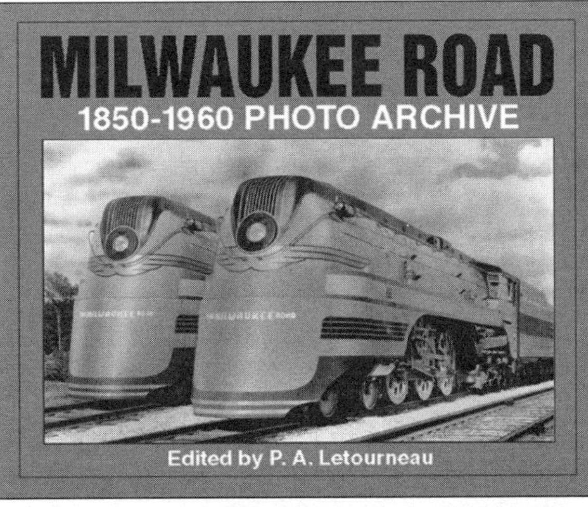

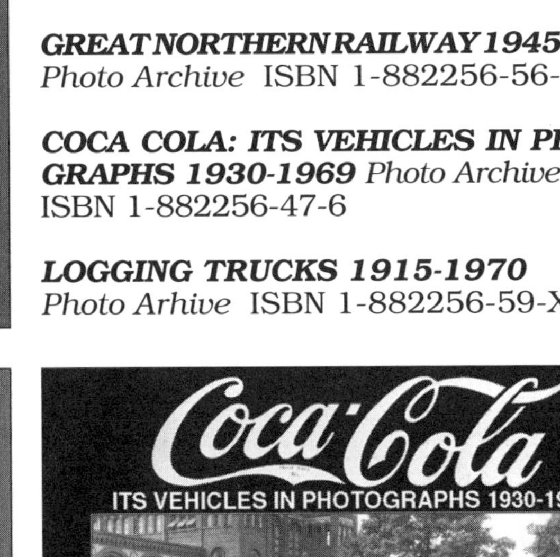

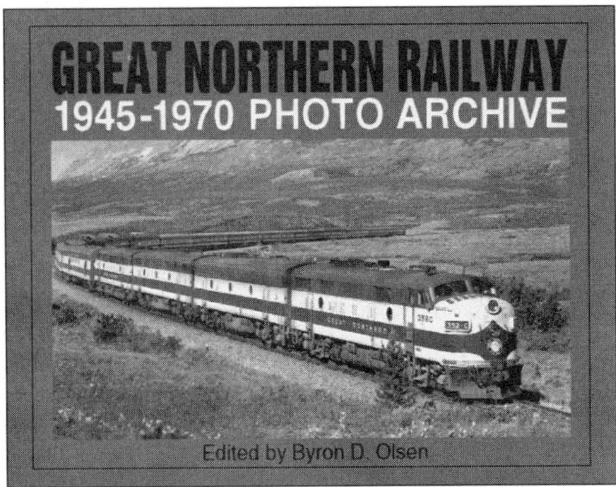